The White Bride

The White Bride

POEMS BY

Sarah Maclay

For Betty & Frank
with love
& a bit of
winter white
Bouquets!
Sarah
'09

UNIVERSITY OF TAMPA PRESS • TAMPA, FLORIDA

Cover art: "O Grave, Where Is Thy Victory" by Jan Toorop. Collection of Rijksmuseum Amsterdam, The Netherlands. Copyright © Rijksmuseum Amsterdam

Photograph of the author by Mark Lipson

Manufactured in the United States of America
Printed on acid-free paper ∞
First Edition

The University of Tampa Press
401 West Kennedy Boulevard
Tampa, FL 33606

ISBN 978-1-59732-041-2 (hbk) ◆ ISBN 978-1-59732-042-9 (pbk)

Browse & order online at
http://utpress.ut.edu

Library of Congress Cataloging-in-Publication Data

Maclay, Sarah.
   The white bride : poems / by Sarah Maclay. -- 1st ed.
      p. cm.
   ISBN 978-1-59732-041-2 (hbk : alk. paper) -- ISBN 978-1-59732-042-9 (pbk : alk. paper)
   I. Title.
   PS3563.A317974W46 2004
   811'.54--dc22   2007049773

Contents

The veils of the sanctuary
Grow luminous in the dark . . .

–David St. John

. . . as if every beautiful thing might also be poison

–Holaday Mason

Ocean in White Chair

The music starts inaudibly, as all music starts. She thinks: tonight there is a hammock, there is memory: they are all glassy rocking, undertow, it is mysterious, nothing in the living room looks wet. They can never talk about it later, they are going to be fools, it is the saddest music, they are smart enough to come back. It is an act of memory, done not with the mind, but with the body. With two bodies they are black water under night; they are the sound the seashell makes, the ear it presses to. They are aqua, ultra. Seaweed flying through like lace. Like stray hair. They pull it back. There is a lie of whispers, but not here. The ocean is the grave of all tears, tears are a memory of ocean. Elegy isn't even elegy, but something deeper: this is what they touch. It is the only music but it is not really sad. They do not cry, they do not have to cry, they are the same wave. Later they cannot talk about it, say the wrong things; make promises they cannot keep or promise not to promise. Anything they say flattens into ribbons, curls away. It *is* this simple: start by asking her about her day, start by asking him about his day, and then begin. Listen with your fingers. The sea is dangerous, they say, but not if you're the sea. What they give each other they will never see in a mirror, they are clothed, it doesn't matter, from the depths of what they're doing they are pausing, they look up, they did not know the ocean looked like this.

Oil on Panel

The sky is wooden. And, beyond the brim of fur that lines their hats, the sea is also made of wood. Because, you see, the wood is a kind of water, a portrait of water, stilled. Things are far from hopeless. And in the same breath—those scalloped hills, those waves of land held in their moment, now appearing dry. And what is that snow, that snow they stand on, edging toward the shore? In their long black coats, in this gray and white landscape— landscape, we say, though air and snow and water are not land— the two men show no sign of cold. Yet we call them frozen. They stand as calm and still as that disc—thin as a communion wafer—disc that seems to sink into the ocean, to dissolve; so white and still now that it doesn't even look like fire. As though we could touch it, look at it. As though it would not, did not burn. What is it the skin of? The tree is the form the water took. The woods were thick with trees. And is it sun or moon? In either case, it neither falls nor rises. Earth has simply turned. And these men, these men are riding on it, thinking it is still, charting the wooden endless horizon, charting the edge of the sea. They might have lived at the rim of the Arctic Circle, might have lived in the 1800s, called themselves explorers, fur traders, surveyors charting the territory of wood. Everything is settled. Mistaking wood for stillness. These men, these frozen men—they might have lived.

Below the Desert

There's the humming, the mosaic of opera vibrating in silence.
There's the loud hush. Mirage, that water, blinds us; windowpanes
the view. Without frame.

Someone is trying to call you and hanging up. Someone with
something to say. It's the buzzing sound you don't quite hear, dry
as sand in the throat.

Look at it: a field of sand, an opera of sand—

Woman Chained to Fire

As if a field of corn is red and orange in the wind, and she raises
her hand to answer a question; then her other hand. Her bare arms
still suspended above the stalks, the cold metal of the cuffs against
her wrists, as the leaves flap about her thighs, tassels exploding
in sparks near her ribs, the hard and swollen ears of corn shifting
their weight in the thrashing wind, her chains attached so far
beneath the tangle of roots that even though they hold to nothing
but flame, she cannot move. The field is a distant one, far from any
house, and the corn, swaying in its night wind, is growing. Her
face is strangely placid. Rusty silk, drying into curls, pushes toward
her mouth, and the corn plants, now persimmon, now electrifying
blue, flicker into each other like a field of tall and narrow wings,
trying to rise altogether into the air, brushing against her back,
flags, the nearly wet slap of their touch, the rush, the sting, how
does she stand, how does she stand it? What is the question?

Scrim

(age of metal, age of speed: the past—

couple of Mercedes Benzes swivel right and pull up to the curb.
Valet opening driver's side, leg of a woman, quivering palm,
chiffon, a breeze, the red of brake lights, motors)

—Ursa Major, Great Bear (like a set of notes)
chime in the dark wind and you must catch them.

Note. Notebook. Book of notes. Book of 3 a.m.
Hum them. Hum the tune set into the sky. Without hammers—

> *(There were many "products."*
> *There were many "clothes."*
> *There were many "interests."*
> *There were many "vacations."*
> *There were many "computers."*
> *There were many "razors.")*

—set into the what-we-call sky. (Words about to be washed away.
A thin thing, their skin, their thin paper.)

A sky filled with garbage. Circuit. Zone. A girdle. An imaginary
path: circle of animals.

Little Sheep, Great Moray, Hail Mary.

Little Lion, Great Snake, Monkey Minor, Ursa Eel, the Lord is
with thee. Hum the new set of animals.

Hum the Great Eel's spanking tail.
(Yellow-throated warbler. Wing. Remains.)

Ursa Driftwood, Ursa Dusk, UnUrsa, Un Mary, UnSkin, "U" will undo the world. Hail Uranium.

Hejira—that word almost erased. When in great danger, you must flee.

Rape

Maybe it is moving like a yellow sea, with corners, so golden under
the late sun, that he has to stop the car. And he stands, now, in
the middle, in this blond field, somewhere in length between a
hundredth and a score. I could say that he discovers, caked in
drying mud, a flat-brimmed sunbonnet: straw beginning to curl,
broad blue ribbon pierced by hat pins. Or that he got in by cutting
the wire of the fence as simply as rope; the few pebbles he stepped
on squashed like grapes beneath his feet. But that didn't happen,
so I will say only that he waded into it, into the field, brushing the
tips of his fingers across the crowns of the plants as their heads rose
past his thighs, and—of the light they reflected—only that it made
the sun too stubborn to set; and he grasped the feathery top of a
stem and stuck it between his teeth and pressed for the shell, the
seed, oil.

Albumen Print from Two Negatives

We're on that road again—road that flies through the path of old-growth sycamores—that country road, the dirt one I'd walk naked on at night—blindfolded and barefoot, feeling my way through the trees, brushing the twigs from my face, and here we are: broad daylight, fallen leaves, leaves as big as your hand and scutting along in the breeze: you know the place. Who cares anymore if you fell from the sky like some great-winged bird? Now you seem to grow from the earth. You hold me, clutch me, pull me, want, I think, to shackle me, consume me—oh, I don't know what you want. I was ready to kiss you, but you pin my shoulders to the earth. You're not malicious, just distracted: this is what I tell myself. You might like to know that it's muddy down here. Puddles form in the ruts on the road, as curved as little saddles. My body is smeared with moistened dirt but I can't help loving the smell, even as you take my clothes like a scavenger and I glance to the side of the road—only inches away, years of green to my left, but I glance back: a brown landscape. Inches away: what I wanted; what I have. You who rip my clothing off may keep it. Keep it. I may walk the road with nothing on, but I will walk it. There is a thing called bitterness. It has a taste.

The White Bride

Alabaster: she glows in the dark. And it is very dark, here in
the drafty chapel, where the ivory satin nearly yellows when
compared to her body, and I would say skin—but there is no
distinction between skin and bone. The veil surrounds her like an
aura—like another source of light—over the appliqué of chenille
and beadwork embroidery. Her face is nearly waxen, upturned—
brooding, it seems—below the white plaster of hair gathered into
a braid and pinned at the nape. She is very still—exceptionally
still—as someone in an adjoining corridor ruminates over the way
whales breed in their sleep. How do they maneuver? In that broad
cradle of water, do they have identical dreams?

And when we leave it is evening, the air damp enough to chill.
No. It is piercingly cold, in spite of the fresh-laid peat, the newly
cut hibiscus—squat and oddly welcoming, a couple of nectarines
about to be planted and the camellia blossoms, whiter than the
stucco behind them, opening their petals, exposing the central bud
. . . and in the wan and graying sky, nothing but the white bride,
stone who does not care for us, shrouded in her veil.

"Let Every Heart"

The blue sash of wind circling the tiny waist of the city, ample and
ample the satin, the keen swishing of leaves, the burnished browns
of dislodged palm piled askew on the walks, the sailing trash,
the cry, the lover's tongue—slowly making its way; the heaving
boughs, the undersides of silver all at once turning together like
birds, the huge relief, the sigh, the way the hair falls to the side, the
fingers turning the scalp to sand, the smell of dope rising up from
the sidewalk—a musk eucalyptus, the sirens, the horns, the bits
of yellow leaves like a stack of *centimes* blown over the street, the
unrelenting sky, these, these ornaments of time, the letting go of
the spine, the held flight of the thousand bougainvillea blossoms
of paper fuchsia and rust, the return, the moment of stillness, the
climbing chords, the lights suddenly off, the parking lot words
of the bantering man in the Chrysler, the lips as expressive as
fingers, the palm debris everywhere like fallen wood, him, it, the
pelvis open like a hinge, the sound exhaled from both bodies, the
sigh beyond color, the steep—the raw—pitch of legato, the face
entirely changed, the face made true, the wind as it spindles the
long limp blinds like a sea of bamboo, oh let me not cease, oh let
me not—let this not—cease, the erupting quiet, the wind, the
snare, the sound of the drum being brushed by sashes, the blue
and terrible sashes, the lush unspoken scream welling up from the
center, lavish, unbearable, this moment, this.

Verse

You unfold the morning caviar, peel the wrapper from a pat of
butter which I'll smear across croissants. You deliver pearls on a
platter. I'll add tiny beads of fish and whirl the string across your
teeth. There. Here's a breath of coffee, here's the crescent of my
thumbnail drawn across your tongue. Here's the grainy meat of
pear, vanilla, coffee beans like berries almost moistening with heat.
Fog pads us from the rush of day, the clam's wings slip open, and
it's not such a long way from one mouth to another. Nuzzle the
morsel inside, examine the surface of the inner shell. That small
orange tongue of lox—slip it into your mouth. Insert the butter
knife between the pages of "A Thousand French Verbs." *Vivre.*
Vernir. Verser. To live, to varnish, to decant, to pour, fill, deposit,
overturn, to shed, to spill. Take this long strand of rain from my
mouth into yours. And wear this strange gray weather like a cloak.

Realism

Flittering in the lit dark: lime, lemon, container of light, portable
star, surface we steal to shine our lips like patent leather, floating
petals, floating jewels, will as transparent as grace, the sound
of time elongating into darkness—a liquid darkness, wrasse,
anemone, sea-horse, kelp, a sheen as translucent as neon, undulant
as vermouth, the sound of a bell just before it rings.

A Dark Colloquy

The words are unimportant: the words do not exist. What is
familiar is closer: the turned face, the hair flicked over the ear. Is
even smaller: the earlobe, exposed, and the small whir of traffic.
Birds like whistles. It's dark enough to hear the clocks tick, the fan's
motor. Inside, outside's small sounds. The small light of breathing.
And the way movement slows. What is breathing? The cup, the
body. What is still? And the lips are closer, the breath in them, and
the mirrors seem redundant—light sources widening the room and
the gathering dark. The long time we can look at each other, and
swallow and breathe, and not go. And the way we remember this
part of the conversation.

The Four Marys

Giotto sends them off in a purple limousine, one driving. Under
the iron clouds of a barren Nevada, thunder lights their way.
Skeptical, they look at the map (oddly glowing on one side, creases
crossing the US of A, long folded), the Van Eyck in the back seat
casting a glance, askance, at her reflection in the rearview, all of
them looking simply for annunciation—not the same as looking
for men, not exactly—and it's not on the map, but maybe they
don't yet know the name of the destination, and anyway, it's a
long drive—this rainless distance, miles of dry, electric air, their
loose veils adrift in the breeze created by movement, as any kind of
movement finally loosens the sticky pastiche of what covers us, and
the moment of our apocalypse can begin.

Grille

As if through glass, through windows, in a café, in the afternoon
or early evening, in June, in June or November, month like a fetish
of gray—a month of water hanging onto itself; until it drizzles,
a month of dulled light—he is seen for a moment, accidentally,
between appointments, in the middle of errands, walking down
steps, the cement steps, say, of an old bank—old enough for
granite, for columns—pulling his keys out of his pocket, or
gripping the small black remote that replaces keys (which you
can't hear the sound of, behind all this glass), and approaching
his car, so that for an instant you see his face unguarded—or as
unguarded as you will see it—and you try to memorize it, but it's
too fleeting, so that now only the back of his head, and maybe the
veins in his arms that you memorized before (the way his fingers
go, his shirt)—or the waiter comes, the waiter comes by and asks
if you've decided, the waiter comes by and asks if you've made up
your mind—

but this is the opposite of confession.

Nude with Violin in Rain

To make the wood sing, and its hollow, to pluck that one sound
from the body, to place it against the thin rail of black wood,
holding it close to the throat, letting it go, while the other hand
finds it in horsehair and bow, oblivious to all the water beating
the forehead, the shoulders, the back of the neck, the breasts the
elbows the shins the whole body, letting that cold water hit like
nails like little tacks in the blur of bad weather, the sound dripping
into the sidewalk; to let the cry come up through the fingers, the
echo drowned, to play anyway, "play"—naked, in public, and let
the voice rise in the strings, in the instrument's ribs, its threaded
ribs—that sound, the sound you must make now or lie—must
you, must you be plaster, be stone?

Trot

A loose translation, not yet quite a gallop, more than a walk: to be literal is to be a little jerky, rider and horse not unified into that smooth flight of sweet aching below the saddle, all feet off the ground at once. Well, another hour goes by. You'll need it. But it gives you the idea—lap slapping against leather or, bareback, the soft hair below the mane, yet it's not a place you can stay for long, breath beginning to move in response to the horse's footsteps— even more involuntary, a quick exhalation, a little fear of being thrown; appetite, the beginning of wind, a canter, a leaning down toward the horse's neck until the motion overtakes us, the scenery unimportant—yet even this is nothing, as the pale summer light retreats: nothing but another loose translation.

Let's Start with Just One Thing We Can Be Sure of

A bell in the window, verdigris, still. How the roses tatter in heat. The branches of a sycamore, twigging into blackness like stiff strands of hair. Desiccated leaves. A light goes on across the street against the outside stairwell where two figures have descended—a loss, somehow, to be lit like this, no longer silhouettes. As though there's some insistence. Here's the truth: I'm lost. Curtains sag across the opened windows like tired bridal veils flung off the face and shoulder—only way to get cool air. Fling them back, exposing the blank retinue of black. The stars somewhere, a matched set of furniture—

Rosamunda, after Antonio

And it's all tires on gravel tonight, cars going too fast between stop
signs—and then stopping again; a lack of mufflers, here some music—
played too loud: several bars of banda, then the throttle of slipping
from gear to gear. This is the street that we take to avoid the street
that gets too crowded. It's everything but night. And so, in the unquiet
final cool of darkness where, to let the air in—just to breathe—I let
the sound in too, I remember that night you filled the apartment with
quiet light, hallucinogenic as a halo, light I sailed in for hours, though
you'd walked down the darkened staircase and out the door, and I
now know that when I sucked the salt from your shoulders, your chest,
when I wanted to go to sleep in your arms—flattering, but strange, we
thought, before even sex—when I buried my mouth into the warmth
of your skin—it was a mouth still looking, rooting for, not only your
cock, your tongue, but that first, elusive breast: it was the mouth of
someone who had found, at last, her mother: impossible to bear. And
so in your leaving, your quiet exit, alone, your finding the way to
unlatch the door, your stepping out onto the concrete porch with the
crippled tomato plants, blanched and sucked-out from the heat, and
the basket marred by remnants of junk mail stuck to the straw from
a rain that happened to fall some months ago, and that strange dark
rose that pushes up from its brief rim of dirt in spite of the lack of any
further rain, and your quiet walk to the car you'd parked along the
curb and the way I didn't hear you drive away that night, as now—
the banda rises again in its lazy turn, executed without a full-throttle
stop— words I don't yet know on a slow ride above the accordion— as
though everything is about to be all right.

In the Rhizosphere

And how quickly

I am only another person to be introduced on the staircase, in the foyer

of this grand room or that . . . when only a week ago, in the dark bed of my ancient room, I woke trying to keep my sounds from the semi-waking consciousness of parents in the room next door, clearing their throats. We'd walked amongst the stones the afternoon before, and on this not-quite morning, stung awake,

> I could not blot out thoughts of *you*, years from now, buried below the sandstone plinth I'd seen in the tiny cemetery—the oldest stone, it seemed, color of dirty cream and swathed with dots of orange lichen, somehow a comfort after the rows of granite engraved in the '90s, or the '70s, as I tripped on the grass because, I realized, like the soil around transplanted trees, the dirt around the graves was still raised slightly—

not an even surface, not a lawn, in spite of the circulating mower manned by someone who knew my father's name, though my father didn't recognize him,

> and as we inspected the headstones of relatives I'd known well as a child, I'd remained unmoved,

> even by the stones set for the ones I'd loved—the ones transported several states—their deaths, by now, a simple fact, their new familial proximity a little quaint, or forced—

or not, finally,
as though the dirt laid rest to feuds.

And now, only this—how I'd lie across the place your bones
would be and curl around the stone I'd designated yours—
how I'd come here, like this, before dawn.

But probably, I thought, you'd designate cremation and get
sprinkled into wind, the sea—some moving element, so that, in
death, you'd vanish as completely—

Yes, it's strange to love a stone, I know, but it was even
stranger to imagine how to love your dust. At least, I
thought, the stone would locate you, at last.

That night my brother's bride to be, who studies what goes on
beneath the soil, described a place that keeps its dead above the
ground in caskets made of glass, and how, one visit, she'd talked
to a widow tending her dead husband's grave. It was covered with
teacups of all kinds, and every day she cleaned them—cleaned
because he had liked tea.

You could leave a cup for him, she said.

Anne B to Henry 8

> I have heard that the executioner is very good.
> And I have a little neck.
> > –Anne Boleyn

I've seen the way you look at her across the room.
I've seen her raise her hand to touch her cheek; I've seen her blush.
I've seen those gray-green eyes, the skin below her neck, the undisguised
*   surprise.*
My dear, I know the signs.
I know your tendency will be to part to other quarters
while the deed is done, take pleasure in your lady's love,
avoid.
Here's what I require of you:
while my head is bleeding, take me by the hair.
Take me to that bowling green that you and I have often walked
and sprinkle me across the grass like Christmas.
Roll my head across the lawn until it hits each pin.
Pick me up then, by the mouth— your fingers that so often slid
between my lips, once more made moist.
Look. Look at this face. This face.
Imagine then the sword has simply done what I myself have thought to
*   do—*
you know, my dear, that she and I have long been friends.
You do remember?
I'll dress for you, as always, in my red below the fur.
I hear there'll be no coffin—you're so kind—but just a box that once
*   held arrows*
like the ones you gave me, with the bow that made such sound.
Fitting, I suppose—only too small, so please
take care to place my head into my hands
once you are done.

Always Another Tonight

Slow, blind, open—drifting sticks, sugar, hands—and even a kind
of drowning is a mystery to the body, a train slipping into soot.
After a decade of cash and ashes, far from the nostalgic dead—
fingers slipping, the raw pillar, legs, the final harsh, abandoned
whinny—a kind of proof, right here: not past, not lost, not ghost.
Here, in this very pew, time is dust, is broken. The old night is
grass. Turn your head. Look at me. Let us not be "the figures."

Irony is the New Black

Outside, they're planting trees: the tick, tick of a tool on soil, a trowel hitting rock. Loam left on the sidewalk in small clumps of black, and now, much later, in the larger black of night, the woman next door is moaning—tick, tick of tool on soil—and moaning shifts the color of the hour, pulling at the thimble of skin. Now all black, all loam resettles, restlessly though, waiting for another wave of sound, as it escalates and scales—the slap, slap of bodies on the other side of the door, loud and urgent enough to enter the kitchen with their sound, the hallway, living room, the staircase splitting its way down the walls that separate these rooms from those, and a cry comes up again, and vanishes; then real crying, the sound of tears, then black—and not the new black, but the old I want to wear: color of sky before stars, before light, under the hollow laughter, under the wince that is the modern face, that night, prior to the sepulcher of bleached light or some prior dawn rehearsing for Rothko, lighting its background of death trees, proper handshakes, sticks. Beyond that light is the old black. And I want to go back.

Leaves

The green brocade, the layers, like a wall of spring—Ophelia, leonine in tub—Bizet a drape of echo on the tile—masculine, the roar, perhaps while shaving, head thrown back—Kurt, Michael, Reed—closer, red, the gold, our clothed bodies, cushions of support—Sebastian, Cleopatra, Howard, Tom—a spell of foliage below, huge, engorged, enveloping, no summer—the tux, the tie, the white shirt on the hanger—Richard—hunger for the shot glass, for the blue pinot—the time this designates, its pages—grigio, bells, white smoke, the crowd now visible if thin—the ever absent diminution of the distances—the wall, the chairs, the carpeting—the visible, the newly nameable—in our midst, in our mist—the teal, the burgundy, the bronze, the fade to ochre, umber, flattening of foreground/background/memory/imagination—Bill, the unknown center of the room—echo chamber of the shell, the hollow 'round which hardness curves—not gone alone—the gone concurrent blond events, the time of velvet hand to glove—as if an opera—as if a song—the tuneless mirror, spill of paper, crushed and wretched stems, the dust—winter a fact, as usual, behind the fall—and what comes after night that is not morning.

(i.m., W. M.—Vancouver, 2005)

The Vehicle

In that room of caramel-hued regret, "the music room," where they
sit on vintage office chairs, apart, in that caramel-colored cell of
wood and sound—the vast feet between them, the small gulping,
glances careful, hurt and sidelong as a cell phone accidentally
switched on—a call gone through, not to an answering voice, but
the way she hears him walking, maybe up a hill—gravel, and small
swatches here and there of music—like a stain—the plaid sound
of a carnival—just its hue, a glimpse of sound, too furtive to be
ambient: this is the look in her eye, this is his hiding, this is her
anger. There they sit on rolling chairs, thunder in the room. She
daggers in a leather jacket open to her bra, her laughs antagonisms
teasing in this interim, this scissory elapse of wind, and he objects.
Nothing can be fudged. This room, this little length has always felt
as though it's lifted from a ship, a wedge of glamour—someone's
curving walls, the damp silk of its fenestration; any moment now,
champagne tucked snugly in its niche of ice and iron while the
guests in black and white drape casually, as at a gala, through the
snaking waves of jazz. And it's the tenor, now, who pierces them.
They find their hands. The fingers rubbing either palm, then
climbing up the wrists—the offered wrists, if nothing else. He
shatters them; he shakes them down, the singer, with his cry—his
plea of hallelujah as the shirt-snaps pop and now the chairs are
rolling closer and the arms are being squeezed and there's no
room for any truth but lips and now the clothes and errors drop
and now—you know, you must be patient—now the blemishes
can faint, the errors can disorganize, the navigation of the wheels
can shift, the whole flimsy ditch can fill with water and dissolve,
because below his song the tenor's voice itself is saying *we don't*

want to look across the room in order to address each other from that
distance as Saint Tomb, vacuous and oral. Emptiness can fill, can
electrify with touch—nerves bright as coral, wheels kicked close,
twisting on dull wax; mouth on mouth: succulent ellipse.

Flight

It is the moment of wind and a growing thunderhead in the desert—thick gray fabric of sky, about to churn. And near the deserted convention rooms of this blind hotel, travelers gather their bags, the foyer decked anew—tables set with a thousand glasses and white, ceramic cups; flatware, chafing dishes; nothing touched. As though an entire bridal party is about to blow in—but hasn't. Water droplets beading the pitchers like sweat on an upper lip. Even the waiters, nowhere to be found. And it's in this moment that the breezes rustle the tablecloths, fresh as skirts. The pressing heat of several days is gone. Tamarisk threading the distance, ocotillo startled into spikes. And the glasses I've worn for the last two years are about to disappear.

Hinge

You see, it's the fabric of the darkest butterfly's wing. And it opens
that way. Closes. Indigo. Vetiver. Velvet. Silk. Old enough now
to have achieved a quiet iridescence. A heart of radium. And this
is the last time it will open upon him, close, open. But neither
of them knows this—for sure. Or they do. They do and it is also
polite, their re-acquaintance here, their adieu, and he is careful
to praise. And she—careful. And the light has fallen, and soon
he will throw candy into the air, like confetti, on crowds, and
later—parades: parades across the bridge, at dusk, at the moment
of grackles, moment of bats, swooping in hordes, and arcing—
visible, invisible—like insects, large, and then the swirl of white
wings over the ashy water near the darkening trees—someone says
they're doves—the birds all following the movement of the water
as though they know where they're going, as though it were a river,
though everyone crossing the bridge refers to it as a lake—and
the owl now, suddenly sweeping toward them, quizzical, piercing,
alone.

Figure in Permanent Field

*There were too many endings. Beginnings grew less clear. And here,
after all, was the second half of things. You won't remember this now,
but later, you knew me. It was in that dream of the other century,
still ahead. Perhaps you had come across me in that strange way of
yours—protective, awkward, intense—even as I worked at the small
desk just beyond the landing. Even as you entered with your flask. And
though you barely spoke, I felt your blessing. You say you never gave
one, but you did. I can tell you now what I was doing in that field,
where you saw me sleeping. It was all I wanted, to be lying there in
white. It was all I wanted for a long time—unless, that is, the kite you
saw suspended from my wrist began, eventually, to lift me. Meanwhile,
I was the counterweight. Meanwhile, I could sleep. But I'd have let it
take me anywhere. It was a chance.*

Black Lake

Still, the black-necked geese convey themselves around it like
confined swans. And we can assume stars, though we cannot see
them. And the color, or its lack, seems right for the temperature
of things, now that it's all a cold glide down. Reflection is an
enterprise of danger—but tonight, the water is kind: a kind of
silence, a kind of lack.

You're out there somewhere, under the moon that must be hiding
here—faith is a long thing to have to keep. And it's too late in the
game—or too early—to get punchy. There's failure. But now the
wind riffling the ragweed with a hint of patience. I gather sage for
you but it doesn't smell.

This is what I'm sure of: the last time I sat near you, there was fog.
How it padded the hotel patio like thoughtful architecture, the
air suddenly grave with a kind of admission. And then that new
sensation on my cheek—and then our two hands nestling like
goslings.

Here, the water gathers at the base of the mountains. Tomorrow
it will be turquoise. In August, Mars will show up in the sky
like a second moon. The narrow sands will fill with tourists and
umbrellas. And I'll return to the last visible messages you sent: the
two tiny shells you placed in my hand before you left. The one tiny
shell I can still find.

Stand of Cut-off Trees

Always, I was smelling things. I had no idea how to behave. My teeth were dull. Some days I woke up unaccountably happy.

For a time, I began to gather things to give to next of kin. For a time, I thought I'd wear the antique lace myself.

I managed to move through houses without damaging the furniture.

People sometimes thought of me as quiet. I don't know what other kinds of sounds I would have made.

Tell me how I could have pretended to be another species.

The sound of the plane is our bodies.
I had never heard it before.

Figure in Permanent Field

*Here's the other thing you didn't see that day, as I lay there in the
stubble, in my long dress: in my other hand, I held a key. You left then,
as the sky began to darken, it is true—but it was not yet evening.
Finally, the thunder. The sky crackled white. The wind came up so
strongly every leaf turned up its skirt—a tree of petticoats, a tree of
white. And so I raised my hand. And in the distance, where the sky
was smeared with gray, I saw an arc—something like a rainbow. Only
white.*

Monochrome, p.m.

It could be June, or January. Snug hood of gray. Sun pries its way in. Must be winter. Last night's dreams have left two marks—two gray hairs, a scratch above the clavicle. As though a gentle cougar . . .

5, 6—chalk on horizontal tiles of gray. Tree shadow—gray on gray. Muffle after muffle. Chrome shines from a Chevy De Luxe, its scoreboard covered with dice. Someone practicing an aria: here's the sound—the tines climb like spokes, like a memory of whirling. What is this allure of silver? Little glint on mud.

Slip outside before the face turns gray.

Gratitude

It would have to be a kind of walking on the ceiling. And outside, a loon. No marshland. Still, four calls. The footsteps, though, too close to be occurring on a floor. Too audible.

Wht. Wht. Wht. Wht. Then nothing.

The calls so measured. Then the sounds of dishes being done.

The water running. Spatulas, maybe. But as though outside—just outside the bedroom window. Someone doing dishes in the yard.

Or maybe not a loon.

Or someone walking up the stairs, perhaps, if stairs were level.

What Keeps Me

The crack at the base of the painting from where it was thrown
and the way the bottom corner of its frame separates—just there.
And is it a very fast and tiny typewriter or moth wings beating
against the closet wall? Or the ticking of a heart?

Landscape crushed like tin foil and the way the iridescent lake is
peeling from it at its borders—like a fallen leaf. The stream shuts
off at midnight as the lake begins to curl around its edges, and the
distant toilet flushing, 5 a.m.

And glaciers, too, sinking into mountains like potato chips. Sheen
of asphalt. Who's a saint? The clock, beating out its tune. Someone
peeing into a large cup.

And is it a very fast and tiny typewriter the stream shuts off at
midnight as the lake begins to curl around the closet wall or moth
wings beating against the distant toilet flushing, 5 a.m.—and the
way the bottom corner of its frame separates. At its borders, its
edges,

the crack at the base of the painting—and glaciers, too, sinking
into mountains shunted to the side in piles like potato chips.
Someone peeing into a large cup and the way the iridescent lake is
peeling from it like a sheen of asphalt. Landscape crushed like tin
foil from where it was thrown—just there.

The clock beating out its tune, like a fallen leaf or the ticking of a
heart. Who's a saint?

Obbligato

It's frazzling as a spectral calypso through the pampas, my pale palomino. I'm drenched—but I deteriorate. One whiff of your mug, laddie, and I low. How about a minesweeper to get me through this overture of rubble? Stirfry up a bit of ivory—I mean ivy. Utter an artichoke or two, as your opulent gramophone pleads with my heartland and I waver snazzily as we dine. Dirty the pitcher. Watch me sweat as you evade. Evict me from my doves, pal—we'll evolve.

For You Who Are Not with Me Who Are with Me

Because you are such a cloth man, I must start with the cloth
report—in this case with our friend in gauzy white on black,
those famous black grapes dripping from her earlobes, dangling in
strands, as she assembles the seating, checking out the room,
while our thin and vibrant friend, in a green frock-that-could-
be-called-a-frock, jokes about her reading glasses as she reads to
us—all smoke and leaves and wood and sex and shining and the
Seine and dusk and our friend/her friend whose mother died and
father died and husband left and son is leaving for college and
who is sparkling now in the awkward embrace of a life she does
not know, in green, in jeans, more fully alive, and our friend all
reds and oranges and peach and freckle-diaphanous-lit on her two
martinis and cackling, eyes jade olives, penetrating, vividly, the air,
and her friend/my friend with the pulled-back hair and the dozen
brothers or so and tonight her friend in specs and our friend whose
husband also left four years ago, her graying hair now shoulder-
length as though she's been allowed to become a girl again as she
smiles with her new and bearded, twinkling friend and his grown
son, and our other friend who loves our (not here) *other* friend but
it was over a year ago or two and she's pulled together in a chic-
er lace brigade (if not brocade) and her hair, all auburn-toned,
allows her to wear her body differently, somehow, with a kind
of now-found stateliness and her friend (who I've only recently
met) is champagne, all joy and frazz—and now, as I turn to the
back, our blond friend who I'd imagined sitting next to tonight
while gazing at you in a mini-skirt, no stockings—only instead
I'm wearing something I didn't need to iron—a blousy film of
longish dress with flecks of fallish flowers, all brown and longer
and black and under it the stockings covered from bottom to top

with flowers, brown and orange, gold, that some have mistaken in
the past, in airports, for tattoos—but you see I can take them off
and wash them—and so (this is where we went tonight) our red-
haired friend is making me walk across the room while lifting my
dress and it's only at the end of the evening that our blond-haired
friend moves closer, breaking into tears because of a migraine so I
manage to cadge a couple of Advil from our friend with the grapes
and after sausage and a beer our blond-haired friend is nearly
glamorous again—a word I shouldn't use, you know, but will—
tossing back her head with the friendly guy in the leather jacket
and glasses who's always smiling, and also with my tall and sylvan
friend (*she* slips two folded paper sonnets into my drawstring bag
but later, when I tease the black silk open, there are only a couple
of pieces of antique lace) and her husband—while below, a crowd
of hundreds jams into the outdoor brick café, twirling scarves
and almost dancing, every age, to hear a young guitarist twanging
out her evening chords and beginning to sing and of course—to
go back to the room for a second—our friend who is playing the
saxophone (though it's been nearly confiscated as a weapon and
someone says it was because of the case—it looked like a gun—but
no, our black grape friend says, no, it was the instrument itself that
set off rumors)—and his forehead, tonight, just beginning to bead
with sweat, his wrists embraced, encircled with, on one, a sleek
tres Western watch, on the other a necklace of brown and wooden
beads, from Africa, I think, but do not know, and tonight he is the
firmest of brown mountains blowing into the lacquered sax—its
brass keys set on top of a horn so silvery it's almost black and the
sound that pours from it is gold and silver and black and black
gold and it hits my neck now, which is where *you* come in—as
my head begins to drop on its hinge and I close my eyes and my
hair, already frowsy, dangles like limp cloth and it's all a river now,

[46]

of our accidents and multiple and singular desires and words and leaves and smoke and dusk and the Seine, all shining, and then the way your hand, right now—descent under water—would have given itself to my neck and the way I would, descent, go under, anywhere with—under flame with—you, even as the high brick walls in back of the terrace, where I'd imagined leaving the crowd with you and leaning into—even as these walls, this turf is guarded by security, in white—and all the secluded benches are taken and even the long, oval pond that is really a fountain reflects the night like a slippery stretch of patent leather, like the most alluring couch, so that I have to dip my hand in now, so that I have to break the surface with my finger—ok, the merest trespass—and *actually*—and let me slide that word around in my mouth and taste it—let me fondle it, if I must live with it—the way it starts with an opening and gets complex in the middle and leaves my tongue with another kind of opening and even though this is not the night we'd hoped for, it is all of this and actually this—*this* is what we've made.

The windows flicker with whips—

black as patent leather. Street shine, headlights and reflection.
Inside, little hums. Shadow of the mirror's edge. Glass reflecting
light. Half the time, there's no way in. Yet there's no sense of
waiting. Of something missing. Someone. It is as though that hole,
once closed, has healed again. Healed over. The mirror simply
bends the light and doubles it. And now I'm looking through
another window into 1950s Paris, 1960s Rome. I could simply
leave the room. And yet another opening is opening. As though
that opening no longer begs.

"Mystery Novel"

Always, he said, one should carry three wigs. He had just removed the one she most associated with his hair. She hadn't seen it coming. Now he looked like a clown. Odd how it most affected the look of his teeth.

He demonstrated the red one. A dyed, greasy look, to wear to the club. Under the glitterball. When midnight is a colander. Little mirrors spreading holes of light. Maybe with specs.

(Meanwhile, every room in the house has been utterly re-arranged—"to create a sense of depth"—even the cast-off lampshades polished and assembled like a collection of vases on top of the bureau—silent, gleaming orbs. And she can't remember the quiet words that join things.)

More Soonest

Something happened. And it blurred. And someone is pounding at the door. We're off-center. Not composed. Composed. Not at rest. I think someone was screaming. There was a door. And the figures were moving. Something was wrong. Couldn't see them. Couldn't see them clearly. Something about "wild hair." Something that looks like an animal. Or a fish. Maybe an octopus. And them—rushing for the door. Two. A bed. A cot. There was a kind of sound I didn't want to hear. What we are doing is necessary. It all happened near the door. Someone was trying to leave. We're not what you think. Or they were about to lift the door. It was where the pillow would be. Giving it all their weight. But the bed had no ending. Simple, really. Had there been a mural on the brick. It was blurry. He was wearing tennis shoes and a belt. Long ago. He was wearing nothing but white. Maybe the paint had been sprayed off. It was black and white. Maybe the paint had been sprayed off.

Or they were pulling it shut.

Portrait of Sunset at Midnight

She loves the way he's promised nothing and fulfilled his promise.
Skirts have stilled—the palms could not be calmer—

sculptural, sepulchral. Perfect May. Even the homeless
woman padding across the street in shirtsleeves.

Palms like sutures, sixties chandeliers
still on in the two apartments with plaster ceilings, windows

open, estuary of metal passing, squarish steel dispensers
of paper—mailbox, "jobs." A prostitute

making her rounds in shorts. The neon curve of sirens—
and it's north, she's facing north,

she knows where north is. Not a hint of wind:
null, null. Like a bell. Knell, knell.

Pare

Strip off the estrogen patch and the world is as gray as the aqua door, across the pool, that refuses to open, sitting like a strip of warped cement reflecting the covered sky; raw as a dream: parking lot, grocery store, everyone guiding their carts with the furious purpose of cars, women's hair pulled out of faces, pupils set like scared dolls' eyes, and then that man clamped on to the empty grocery cart that's skidding, horizontal, off its wheels toward the door that will open in the blink of an electric eye (face a spasm) (all in a matter of seconds)—and when I enter the store, a woman holding a clipboard asks if *I'm* all right.

So maybe this is a way not to lie—like the woman online who says after her *heart chakra was opened* she could not stop weeping. As though we should.

A screen in every parlor like a huge, blank eye.

Subvert

Below the violin of fern, uncurling; under the timothy, beneath
the splitting fans of birds of paradise, their wide embrace, and
below the tall stems of grass we suck but do not call by name, and
the sprouting weeds; under the grove of avocado, waxy leaves of
orange trees, needles of pine feathering into a stately procession,
aloe fingers jutting up; below the hundred lawns too bright with
water—tidy emerald squares, and under, also, awkward spikes
of newly planted palms, under the strip of topaz braceleting the
shore—yes, that too—and below, even, dandelion leaves, felled
narcissus stalks, the narrow calligraphy of orchid stems, and under,
even, limestone, under moss, beneath the wounds of kelp, below
the forests, larch and cottonwood, beneath the fields of deep
alfalfa: under green—these brackets, green erupting catchers of
sun—under the new, the lurid, under the celebrating—thing we
cannot know, the mad array of urgencies and tanglings—roots, the
roots and what is below, and how we cannot hear them speak.

Cassandra: Engraving in Red & Blue

Everyone in the restaurant, he says, is welcome to join in—to scream at the same time as the swarthy, mustached, balding man, near a pile of dishes, just outside the metal port-holed kitchen doors (whose head is being massaged with a red and meaty sauce)—everyone is invited to scream, to drown out his scream, to keep him, as it were, company. This is all explained to her in detail, casually, as the carefully appointed diners, all magnificently calm, sit at their tables in the whitewashed rooms. And then once, he says, the thin sword is wiped clean (and depending on her answers—

How I wish it were otherwise. How I wish I could tell you that there were secret places in the city where, if we were able to perfect the art of getting lost, roads would open onto sudden lakes—where emerald was the name of grass and sand was iridescent, almost liquid, almost breath. Where the wind had been arranged in little bursts. Where the secret choreography that joined us could be viewed—

because, I'll tell you, we could see it—we could see this other story. We were bloody tired of swords. How I wish I could say that when we got up we spent entire days inhaling so completely that our bodies filled with sky.

Ocean without Figures

And now all sound is liquid, settling into the curve of a shell,
filling it—the long, curling funnel opening into sand—and it's
night, or the cusp of dawn, the ocean calm as a lake at the shore,
the smell of the sea opening like fog across the basin for miles, as
if fog could be smelled, as if it carries with it memory: a kind of
body, a kindness, a body awake—

nothing hurts. And all this empties into the necessity of fog:
a vanishing, and the notes, all played, all crafted in tic-tack
Victorian, drop. Much too well we have settled. The unknown,
the hidden, comfort. Not an embrace, but bigger. The vague
obliterates the specific; forgets it, happy, relieved.

Here is the morning estuary—for a moment, beyond fear. And the
ear drinks like a cup as if all sound were ocean, and this cupful,
all we hear—as it sets the tiny bones in motion, sticks in a stream,
and the larger ones, buried far below the sand—the bones that can
only dance—

The Blueberry Field

Maybe night had fallen across the field like a hail storm and stayed, maybe it can be sucked on now, maybe it's sweet—maybe a layer of fog coats each small plumpness, beckoning, like a promise of relief: tiny pods of ripe cool, as he stands surrounded by the navy-dark scalloping of wild growth—over and over as if a child had repeated a word until it became a sound: he crouches by the fruit, examines it.

Day hangs out of its pocket, limp as a rag, water on the verge of bursting from the sky. And in the bright heat, everywhere, the berries. He has never stood in a field of berries before. He has never stood above two hundred thousand bodies, buried twenty feet below. And his standing is not tall.

The others have scattered, the boom man, the cinematographer. Ovens. Ovens were near, then buried. It's hot. He leans close to the fruit. He cannot pick it.

Gun Powder on Paper

And where are we now? Remembering how fine it all is, how remote from something that can kill, as, in a moment, one distraction and the glass plate doesn't make it, as we had intended, to the credenza, and we're surprised by the shattering sound when we let go, the mess of shards on the floor. It's over. Ready for dustpan and broom and so little regret—something to clean. A reason to get on our knees, to attend to the wood below our feet. Something coheres. And now there's a pattern. Now there's a past.

Stone

Someone has etched the word: stone. Someone has felt it.
Someone has seen it lying in a field. All other words, after this,
must be measured against it—the scarves and ribbons of flying
sunset, the baubles worn to the fair—all the assumptions of love,
all the anxieties over its absence. My dear, it's time for the ribbons
to drop, as the opera entirely disappears. And this is all right. The
stone is smooth and weighty. And imperfect.

The Night Roses

And then I could feel their strange weight, wet as night as they fell
from her hands, even the stems flush with scent and dew—and
in the center of this large bouquet, too large to hold—even the
cabbage a too-large rose, even its leaves now petals—as every daily
thing is remembered and fondled as a rose—even the folded night,
even the silence of its singing.

Even its dark song.

The Night Cloth

There is always the path back to the place you began, but this time, take another. You have been given the colors of a Vermeer, made in muted light. They are what twilight does to wheat and shadow. And then the man below you, in his apartment, does a kind of singing—as though he is making song with his fingers as they drum a tabletop. As soon as you name this color gold, it looks like ultramarine or even distant knapweed or even a part of the ocean. The dripping rain on the rooftop is now as random as the click of the second hand heard between the *shhh-shhh* of passing cars. But really, anyway, there's no *where were we*. The cars interrupt the darkness with their splashes of sudden, repeated white. There's a kind of rhythmic humming now from below, as though the voice, or several voices, run, again and again, into a wall, insistent, and the walls themselves are ticking—or is it the heater, or is it the rain. Something apparently wants to chant—will use anything to chant. And you—where do you think you're going.

Notes

The Charles Baudelaire excerpt that appears on the dust jacket of the hardback edition is quoted by Michael Benedikt in his introduction to *The Prose Poem–An International Anthology* (Dell, 1976) from Baudelaire's "preface to his collection *Petites Poèmes en Prose* (later issued as *Le Spleen de Paris*)."

The lines quoted as opening epigraphs are from David St. John's *The Face*, poem "XXXVIII" (HarperCollins, 2004), and Holaday Mason's poem "The Man Who Went to Paris," used by permission of the authors.

Many of these poems have muses, in addition to the live ones, in the form of other works of art—musical, visual, literary—or myth, ritual, cultural artifact, dream, historical fact.

"Ocean in White Chair": after Gorecki's third symphony.

"Oil on Panel": under the influence of Caspar David Friedrich's "Moonrise."

"Woman Chained to Fire": after a *Carta de Loteria* used as a record cover, B-side.

"Albumen Print from Two Negatives": Leda and Jacob hover about the edges.

"Let Every Heart": the title comes from "Joy to the World," traditional Christmas carol. Centimes are tiny French coins. Bougainvillea is pronounced *boo-gan-VEE-ah*.

"A Dark Colloquy": under the spell of Jane Mead.

"The Four Marys": after Nelson de la Nuez's print "Virgins Looking for Saviors."

"Nude With Violin in Rain": apologies to the mannequin in front of the pawnshop on Gardner; meanwhile, still under the spell . . .

"Anne B to Henry 8": the epigraph is part of the public record of Anne Boleyn's writings—in this case, one of her last. She was noted, apparently, for her sardonic wit. Research tells us that she was initially buried, as noted, in a box that had once been a container for arrows. It was too small to accommodate her head.

"Rosamunda, after Antonio": English folklore has it that Rosamund Clifford (1150–1176), mistress of King Henry II, was kept in a secret bower surrounded by a maze of paths penetrable only by a silver thread. During Henry's time away, at war, his queen, Eleanor, did away with the knight left behind to protect the "Fair Rosamund," and then forced her to choose between death by poison or by the blade. (She chose poison, we're told, under duress.) Cervantes builds on and reconfigures this myth in *Persiles y Sigismunda* (1616), in this case making his Rosamunda an over-amorous figure, banished from England because of her robust sensuality, and chained, on a ship, to the slanderous Clodio. Her behavior is contrasted with the extreme chastity of the female heroine. As the characters in this novel make a pilgrimage by sea from the "barbaric" northern lands southward, in order to find a "spiritual home," a fading Rosamunda pursues the chaste Antonio across a barren winter landscape, and when he rebuffs her, she dies of what T. L. Darby calls "unfulfilled lust and remorse for her past life, and is buried at sea, as if the ocean could cool her ardor." (See Karen Lucas's writings on Rosamunda, for more.)

It's worth noting that Pre-Raphaelite painter John Waterhouse's portrait "Lady by the Water" has been linked to both the "Fair Rosamund" story and, more commonly, to Tennyson's "Lady of Shalott," based on the Arthurian legend in which the "lovely" Elaine, in unrequited love with Sir Lancelot, leaves her tower, takes a boat into the water and dies, singing, of a broken heart, essentially freezing to death as the boat drifts into Camelot.

For an examination of the psychological dynamics graphically enacted in this further update of the love- or lust-lorn, see Howard M. Halpern's work on attachment hunger and the double-edged power of the fusion experience.

"In the Rhizosphere": after Jill Clapperton's tale of coming across the burial traditions and mourning practices referenced at the end of the poem, on the islands of Samoa.

"The Vehicle": after Leonard Cohen via Jeff Buckley. Also, thanks to Nik de Dominic and *Void Magazine* for providing revision inspirations.

"Figure in Permanent Field": after "Brugge," by Franz Wright, and "Grass Widow," by Cecilia Woloch—as though the figures in these poems, which were composed many years apart and without reference to one another, were the same—and could speak.

"For You Who Are Not With Me, Who Are With Me": apologies to Frank O'Hara. Thanks to MOCA and everyone gathered there over two seasons of Nightvision.

"More Soonest": after Rocky Schenk's "Suddenly."

"Subvert": *vert* is "green" in French.

"Cassandra . . .": She who was given the power of clairvoyance, and the curse that no one cared.

"The Blueberry Field": Sobibor, in the Lublin district of Poland, was a Nazi extermination camp in operation from May of 1942 to October of 1943. Prisoners were taken there by rail; the gas chambers were fed by exhaust fumes from the diesel engines of tanks. The estimate in the poem may be low by about 60,000. After an uprising during which about 300 prisoners escaped, the camp was bulldozed over and replanted with trees. As recently as 2001, researchers discovered seven mass graves at this site.

"Gun Powder on Paper": after Ashbery, after Ed Ruscha.

"Stone": in the sway of Sophie Cabot Black.

"The Night Roses": for Barbara Blatt, who dreamed of being handed a similar, but even more various, bouquet.

"The Night Cloth": after Transtromer, after receiving gifts.

Acknowledgements

Deepest thanks to the editors and publishers of the following publications, in which these poems first appeared individually:

The American Poetry Review: "Leaves" and "The Vehicle"

Askew: "A Dark Colloquy"

FIELD: "The White Bride," "Grille," "The Blueberry Field," "Gratitude," "Hinge," "Black Lake," and "Stand of Cut-off Trees"

Gulf Coast: "Pare"

Hunger Mountain: "Flight"

The Journal: "The Four Marys" and "Let Every Heart"

The Laurel Review: "Ocean in White Chair" and "More Soonest"

The Los Angeles Review: "Scrim" and "Rape"

LUNA: "Subvert"

Media Cake: "Anne B to Henry 8" and "What Keeps Me"

mid)rib: "Always Another Tonight"

Ninth Letter: "The Night Cloth"

Parthenon West Review: "Irony is the New Black," "Gun Powder on Paper," "Realism," "Nude With Violin in Rain," and "Below the Desert"

Ploughshares: "Oil on Panel"

Poemeleon: "Ocean without Figures"

poeticdiversity: the litzine of Los Angeles: "The Windows Flicker with Whips," "For You Who Are Not with Me Are with Me," and "The Night Roses"

Poetry Flash: "Cassandra: Engraving in Red & Blue"

Poetry International: "Woman Chained to Fire," "Albumen Print from Two Negatives"

Scripter.net: "Stone"

So Luminous the Wildflowers: "Verse"

Swink: "Portrait of Sunset at Midnight"

Washington Square: "Trot" and "Let's Start With Just One Thing We Can Be Sure Of"

"Ocean in White Chair" and "Let Every Heart" were reprinted in *Poemeleon. Scripter.net* reprinted "Gun Powder on Paper" and "The Night Roses." *The Squaw Valley Review* anthologized "Black Lake."

Thank you to the Albert & Elaine Borchard Foundation for a fellowship that allowed me to work on a group of these poems at the Tomales Bay Workshops.

Thank you to my first listeners and responders: Tony Barnstone, Marjorie Becker, Elena Byrne, Molly Bendall, Jeanette Clough, Brendan Constantine, Mark Fox, Dina Hardy, Robert Hass, Holaday Mason, Louise Mathias, Jane Miller, Harryette Mullen, Jim Natal, Carl Phillips, Sharon Olds, David St. John, Jan Wesley, Cecilia Woloch, C. D. Wright, Brenda Yates, Dean Young, and the many poets at Squaw '06 and Tomales Bay '05.

Thanks to Chris Beckman, Bruce Boston, Fred Dewey, Adam and Lisa Gross, Mark Kemble, David Killoran, Fred Moramarco, Judith Pacht, The Potts family, Sheryl Rabinovich, Charles Rial, Linda and Miguel Sandoval, Susan Shilladay, Gail Wronsky, and to others already mentioned, for keeping me housed, and involved with the tasks of teaching and editing, during the period in which these poems were written.

Special thanks to the Rijksmuseum, and in particular to Anna van Lingen and Cecile van der Harten, for allowing us to use Jan Toorop's 1892 image on the cover.

Ongoing thanks to the folks at Tampa, especially Richard Mathews, for his patience, good judgment, and fine design skills, and for his sense of humor. Thanks to Sean Donnelly for his consistently fine and dependable work and forbearance.

Thanks to Michael Child for making the sound recordings of these poems, and to Stephanie Prodromides, for proofing and for listening to the work as a whole.

Special thanks to Mark Fox.

Thank you and *abrazos* to my students!!

About the Author

Sarah Maclay received the Tampa Review Prize for Poetry for her first book, *Whore*, which was published by the University of Tampa Press in 2004. Her poems have appeared in periodicals such as *APR, FIELD, Ploughshares, Pool, Lyric, Hotel Amerika, Solo,* and *ZYZZYVA*, and are included in *The Best American Erotic Poems: 1800 to the Present* (Scribner, 2008). Her essays and reviews have been published in *The Writers Chronicle* and *Poetry International*, where she serves as book review editor. She received a Special Mention in *Pushcart Prize XXXI* and a fellowship from the Albert and Elaine Borchard Foundation, and is also the author of three limited edition chapbooks: *Shadow of Light* (Inevitable Press), *Ice from the Belly* (Far Star Fire) and *Weeding the Duchess* (Black Stone Press). A native of Montana, she earned degrees from Oberlin College and Vermont College, and has taught at USC and FIDM. She lives in Venice, California, where she periodically serves as a poet-in-residence at Beyond Baroque. She is currently a visiting assistant professor at Loyola Marymount University.

About the Book

The White Bride is composed in Adobe Garamond Pro types based on the sixteenth century roman types of Claude Garamond and the complementary italic types of Robert Granjon. They were adapted for digital composition by Robert Slimbach in consultation with colleagues including type historian and designer Steven Harvard, letterform expert John Lane, and Adobe's Fred Brady. Slimbach and Brady have written that Garamond's "roman types are arguably the best conceived typefaces ever designed, displaying a superb balance of elegance and practicality." The book's title font is Herman Zapf's Zapfino, a digital type based on an alphabet the famous typeface designer and calligrapher penned in 1944. The section marker is a P22 Arts and Crafts ornament by Richard Kegler, derived from a Roycroft book decoration of Dard Hunter and released by the P22 Type Foundry of Buffalo, N.Y. The book, printed on acid-free natural Finch Opaque Vellum, was designed and typeset by Richard Mathews at the University of Tampa Press.

POETRY FROM THE UNIVERSITY OF TAMPA PRESS

Jenny Browne, *At Once*

Jenny Browne, *The Second Reason*

Richard Chess, *Chair in the Desert*

Richard Chess, *Tekiah*

Richard Chess, *Third Temple*

Kevin Jeffery Clarke, *The Movie of Us*

Jane Ellen Glasser, *Light Persists**

Kathleen Jesme, *Fire Eater*

Steve Kowit, *The First Noble Truth**

Lance Larsen, *In All Their Animal Brilliance**

Julia B. Levine, *Ask**

Julia B. Levine, *Ditch-tender*

Sarah Maclay, *Whore**

Sarah Maclay, *The White Bride*

John Willis Menard, *Lays in Summer Lands*

Kent Shaw, *Calenture**

Barry Silesky, *This Disease*

Jordan Smith, *For Appearances**

Jordan Smith, *The Names of Things Are Leaving*

Lisa M. Steinman, *Carslaw's Sequences*

Marjorie Stelmach, *A History of Disappearance*

Richard Terrill, *Coming Late to Rachmaninoff*

Matt Yurdana, *Public Gestures*

* Denotes winner of the Tampa Review Prize for Poetry